INTRODUCTION

Julius Caesar was stabbed to death in March 44 BC. He had no son, and in his will named his great-nephew as his heir and adopted him as his son. The eighteen-year-old Caesar Octavian was launched into a political career, and into the civil wars which raged for thirteen years as factions fought for power at Rome. In 31 BC Octavian crushed his last rival, Mark Antony, at the battle of Actium off north-west Greece.

In 27 BC he chose to restore the Republican constitution which had been extinguished by the civil wars, and accepted the name Augustus offered to him by the Senate. Through his accumulation of traditional magistracies and powers his position was unrivalled, and he ruled Rome as emperor for forty-four years. He established a dynasty, and, though he was thwarted several times by death or accident in his choice of a successor, he was finally succeeded by his stepson Tiberius in AD 14.

A description of Augustus has been preserved in the biography written by Suetonius in the early second century. 'Throughout his life, his appearance was distinguished and graceful. He did not dress extravagantly and cared so little about his hair that several barbers worked furiously on it at the same time. His beard was either trimmed or shaved while he continued reading or writing. He had clear bright eyes..few teeth, which were small and dirty...his hair was yellowish and slightly curly, his eyebrows met and his nose jutted out and then turned inwards. He was neither dark nor fair, and was rather short, but with well-proportioned limbs. On his body were spots, birthmarks and callouses caused by excessive use of the strigil. He sometimes limped and suffered generally from a weak constitution. Unable to endure heat or cold, he always wore a hat outdoors and in winter wore a woollen vest...' (*Augustus*, 79-82).

The portraits of Augustus hardly reproduce this description of his features, because they were not intended to convey his physical appearance, but to present him as the embodiment of his own political ideals. They were part of an extensive imperial propaganda campaign controlled by Augustus himself. His image appeared all over the Roman Empire, and more portraits of Augustus have survived than of any other emperor.

The image created by Augustus for his subjects stemmed from a long tradition of portraits of rulers and public figures in the Classical and Hellenistic worlds. Traditions of portraiture in the Roman Republic also influenced Augustan portraits, both those of members of the imperial family and those of private citizens. The conventions governing the granting of portraits to individuals in Greece and at Rome also helped to determine the history of portraiture under Augustus.

Fig.1 Alexander the Great wearing the aegis of Zeus

RULER-PORTRAITURE IN THE GREEK WORLD

In democratic city-states such as Athens, where at the close of the sixth century BC tyranny had been overthrown in favour of direct participation in government by all adult male citizens, strict rules were observed concerning the dedication of portrait statues to leading public figures.

A different attitude to portraiture existed on the fringes of the Greek world in areas like Lycia, Caria and Macedonia, where portraits of rulers, their consorts and their kinsfolk were an accepted feature of political and religious life.

Of these dynastic states, Macedonia had the strongest influence on the development of ruler portraiture in Hellenistic Greece and Rome. The Macedonian kings, of mixed ethnic origin, valued Greek culture highly; furthermore, by 338 BC, Philip II had achieved by military and diplomatic means domination over the Greek city-states. He subsequently commissioned the Greek sculptor Leochares to make gold and ivory statues of himself and other members of the Macedonian royal family. These were set up in a circular monument in the panhellenic sanctuary at Olympia, where the Greeks celebrated the Olympic Games. Although the statues were the work of a Greek, the monument may have offended the Greeks, who had refrained from setting up portraits of living persons in a place sacred to the gods.

Several Greek cities whose citizens had received favourable peace terms from Philip II set up statues of their new ruler; others did so as a prudent gesture of appeasement.

Philip's ideals of Greek cultural supremacy and unity under Macedonian leadership were continued after his death by his son Alexander (336-323 BC), who led the Greeks in a crusade to destroy the Persian empire. Alexander advanced rapidly eastwards, conquering a vast mass of territory, much of which was superficially hellenised on 'liberation' from Persian rule. Alexander controlled the form of his portrait by appointing distinguished Greek craftsmen to portray him in various media: Lysippos for bronzes, Apelles for paintings and Pyrgoteles for engraved gems.

After a brilliant military career Alexander died at the age of thirty-two. His premature death inspired romantic views of his personality and achievements: to the Romans he symbolised military conquest, and he remained a model for Roman generals and emperors who wished their portraits to convey their military achievements. For the Greeks, he served as a model of kingship; the debt to Alexander is apparent in the portraits of his immediate successors, his generals and associates, who ruled his divided empire after his death in 323 BC.

Some portraits of the young Alexander express his Greek upbringing (his tutor was Aristotle, foremost Greek philosopher of the day), and reflect the period of pan-hellenic unity in the war against Persia (fig.1). However, most surviving portraits of Alexander reflect his posthumous deification. These vary in style and in the treatment of their subject according to the time and place of manufacture: the most important of the latter was Alexandria in Egypt, where his tomb lay (fig.2). Portraits on coins also appeared after his death as some of his successors sought to justify their claims to parts of his empire, for instance Ptolemy I at Alexandria (fig.3a + b).

Since Alexander had tried to promote a stereotyped image of himself, many features of his portrait could be reproduced by his imitators. Among personal characteristics may be reckoned his hairstyle, the *anastole*, in which uplifted front locks fell gracefully to either side of a central parting; the position of the head, turned to one side and up; a melting gaze in his eyes; the swollen care-worn appearance of his brow and his habit of leaving his cheeks unshaven.

Certain gestures, symbols and items of clothing reveal the likening of Alexander to various gods, both Greek and oriental. The enormous eyes gazing up to heaven and the star that appeared on the portraits were marks of deification; some early portraits showed him in the aegis of Zeus (fig.1), while posthumous portraits had ram's horns over his ears (fig.3a) - a characteristic of the god Zeus Ammon, his reputed divine father. The ram's horns often appeared with the thunderbolt and aegis of Zeus. A chariot drawn by elephants, or an elephant-scalp, recalled the god Dionysos, conqueror of the east, and evoked Alexander's triumphs in India (fig.3b).

Taken either singly or together, these attributes often appeared in the portraits of Alexander's successors and in those of Roman generals and emperors who wished to emulate him.

Portraits of living monarchs were first put to political use after 305 BC (fig.4), when some of the successors took the title 'king' and placed their own portrait on coins to proclaim this assumption of the royal position. This use of the coin portrait spread rapidly and is the most impressive feature of Hellenistic coinage, from north Africa to India.

The personal features of Alexander's portraits continued to influence Hellenistic ruler portraiture (fig.5), but the use of divine attributes of Alexander and other divinities became rare after the third century as the kings preferred to stress their regal aspects through a prominent display of the diadem (fig.19c), the symbol of royalty. There were changes in fashion too: in about 200 BC the kings of Macedon, Bithynia and Pontus chose to have

Fig.2 Posthumous portrait of Alexander from Alexandria. 2nd Cent. BC

Fig.3a Alexander wearing the ram's horns of Zeus Ammon; minted by Lysimachus

Fig.3b Alexander wearing the elephant's scalp of Dionysos; minted by Ptolemy I

Fig.4 Seleucus I wearing symbols of Poseidon and Dionysos
Fig.5 Mithradates VI of Pontus wearing a lion's scalp. 120-63 BC

a beard instead of a clean-shaven chin like Alexander. By the first century BC, some traditions of ruler portraiture had moved away from the Alexander type: a Parthian contemporary of Augustus, Phraates IV, looked more like an oriental despot than a Hellenistic king (fig.6a). Some kings saw their portraits become stylised as their power became feeble, for example in Ptolemaic Egypt or Seleucid Syria (fig.6b). Elsewhere, too, there were portraits which owed little or nothing to Alexander: 'that hairy youth', Juba I of Numidia, was shown as a barbarian king, while Tarcondimotus of Cilicia, given the title of king by Antony in about 35 BC, was portrayed in a style akin to that of the traditional portraits of Roman aristocrats (p. 8 fig.6c-d).

ROMAN ATTITUDES TO PORTRAITS

In Republican Rome, as in some Greek city-states, the portrayal of a person's features seems to have been associated with aspirations to monarchy or tyranny.

In some cities, however, statues were dedicated to those who had given exemplary service to the state. In 510 BC, the Athenians set up statues on public land to Harmodios and Aristogeiton, who had slain the tyrant Hipparchos. These statues were idealised: they did not portray the personal features of the tyrannicides. The honoured individuals could be identified from their names, which were inscribed on the base of the monument, and from the pose of the figures, shown in the act of assassinating the tyrant.

Idealised statues are now generally associated with Greek notions of the perfection of the human body. On public monuments, however, idealised figures could be combined with the names of honoured individuals to inspire others to live up to the high standards of those commemorated in the monument. In a similar way, some modern war memorials combine an idealised figure of an unknown soldier with a list of names of individual soldiers honoured by the monument.

Fig.6a Phraates IV. c.33-2 BC

Fig.6b Antiochus XIII of Syria. 69-64 BC

Fig.6c Juba I of Numidia 60-46 BC

Fig.6d Tarcondimotus of Cilicia. c.35 BC

Fig.7 Column surmounted by statue of Lucius Minucius

Idealised portraits were also known in Republican Rome: statues in the Forum were awarded to the Coruncanii brothers, one of whom was put to death by Teuta, queen of the Illyrians, during a dangerous diplomatic mission in 230 BC. These statues were only three feet high, and clearly had an honorific significance.

Because of their political importance, the dedication of public statues was strictly regulated by the Senate and later by the popular assembly. Pliny says that the first such popular award was made in 439 BC to Lucius Minucius, who saved the city from famine through his management of the corn supply (fig.7). The erection of such statues was supervised by the censors. In 184 BC, the reactionary censor Cato tried unsuccessfully to ban public statues of women in Italy, and in 158 BC the same magistrates removed from the Forum statues set up without proper approval.

The prominence of public portraits made them vulnerable to the consequences of sudden political change. Statues of Marius Gratidianus had been set up in all districts of Rome, but these were pulled down when Sulla entered the city in 82 BC, as Gratidianus was the nephew and active supporter of Sulla's bitter rival, C. Marius. Statues of unpopular Roman emperors who suffered *damnatio memoriae* (official, posthumous condemnation by the Senate) were also melted down, mutilated or recarved. The younger Pliny described with relish the destruction of golden statues of the emperor Domitian (AD 81-96): 'It was a delight to hurl that proud face to the ground, to molest it with the sword and savage it with axes, as if blood and pain would follow from every blow. There was no restraining anyone's joy or happiness after so long: it seemed a kind of revenge to see those bodies mangled, those limbs chopped off, those savage dreadful images thrown to the flames and melted down....'

TRADITIONAL ROMAN REPUBLICAN PORTRAITS

The Republican portraits that survive belong mainly to the first century BC, and fall into two groups, the traditional and the heroic.

The traditional portraits are of citizens possessing the *ius imaginum*, the customary right to portraits. Ex-magistrates and their descendants were allowed to keep wax copies of their ancestors' death masks, arranged in groups connected by red lines to form a family tree, in cupboards in the courtyards (*atria*) of their houses (fig.8).

It was believed that the surviving portraits in stone, on gems (fig.9) and on coins were derived directly from such masks; their severe lines and the rendering of every blemish and wrinkle of the skin seemed to make them accurate representations of noble Romans on their deathbeds. It has recently become clear, however, that these characteristics are stereotypes which are reproduced in portraits of different persons. Most likely they belong to the stylistic

Fig.8 Statue of a Roman carrying two portrait busts of his ancestors. Late 1st century BC

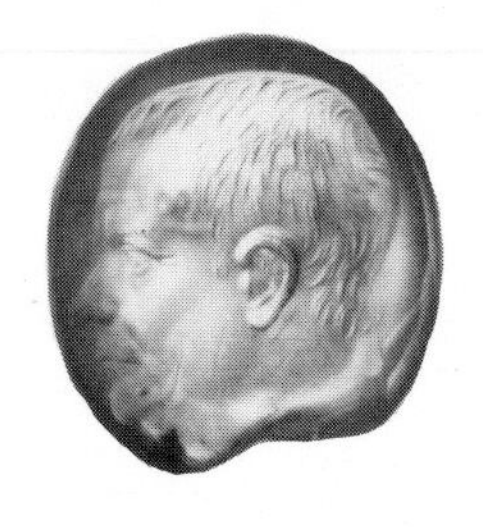  

Figs.9abc Roman gem portraits of the 1st Cent. BC

repertoire of a particular artist or workshop of sculptors. The later development of this type (p.36) also suggests that such portraits were not individually authentic, but were idealisations embodying the traditional values of the old patrician families. The masks were worn at funerals by those members of the family of mature years who bore the closest resemblance to the subjects of the masks, in order to impress upon their junior siblings and offspring the need to perpetuate the family line, to live up to the noble traditions of their ancestors, and to act bravely on behalf of the state.

THE HONOURING OF MILITARY LEADERS

Portraits that reflected the exploits of individuals, glorifying their subjects rather than inspiring others, became familiar to the Romans through military expansion into the Greek-speaking areas of southern Italy and Sicily in the third century BC. Greek works of art looted from conquered cities were displayed at Rome in the triumphs awarded to successful generals. At first, such treasures were dedicated to the gods who had helped bring victory. Later, however, they were displayed in porticoes built by the triumphant generals in the area of the Circus Flaminius (a poor quarter of the city). The generals also commissioned Greek artists to make copies of famous masterpieces for display in their own homes. Some Roman aristocrats acquired a taste for Greek art and chose to have themselves portrayed by Greek artists.

When Roman generals appeared in the eastern Mediterranean, they were hailed by many Greeks as the successors to the Hellenistic kings (p.4). This reception was significant for the development of public portraits in the later Republic. The generals were obliged to play two roles: at Rome, they were expected to assume a Republican modesty, whereas some of them were honoured almost as gods by the Greeks.

The portraits of these figures can reflect the difference between their status at home and abroad. The statue of a Roman general from Tivoli, for instance, (fig.10) is carved in Pentelic marble, almost certainly by a Greek

Fig.10 Statue of a Roman general from Tivoli. c.75–50 BC

Fig.11 Posthumous portrait of Pompey the Great

sculptor, who portrayed the subject in heroic semi-nudity. The appearance of the torso contrasts sharply with the head, which has the qualities of austerity and merciless attention to detail of the traditional Roman portrait (p. 8). As he was forbidden to appear at Rome in anything other than civilian dress, the general's military cuirass has been discreetly relegated to serve as a support for a leg of the statue.

The exploits of Roman military leaders such as Sulla (in the eighties BC) set the pace for such developments while the scale of their operations changed dramatically with the appointment of Pompey in 66 BC as commander with responsibility for the eastern Mediterranean. Pompey, already awarded the name 'Magnus' (the Great) in his twenties, later founded new provinces, made and destroyed kings, and was described in dedications made in Asia Minor as the founder and saviour of cities. His portraits, and the name, show how he consciously modelled himself on Alexander. The portraits have similar personal characteristics - the *anastole*, the melting gaze of the eyes and unshaven cheeks (fig.11). The point of these features will not have been missed by the Romans, to whom the features of Alexander were familiar: at least seven portraits of him are known to have been on display at Rome in the first century BC.

Surviving portraits of Julius Caesar, dictator at Rome from 48 until his assassination by Republicans in 44 BC, show that, unlike his former rival Pompey, he

Fig.12 Gem portrait of Julius Caesar. c.42 BC
Fig.13a Julius Caesar. Jan-Feb.44 BC
Fig.13b Julius Caesar; coin of Nicaea

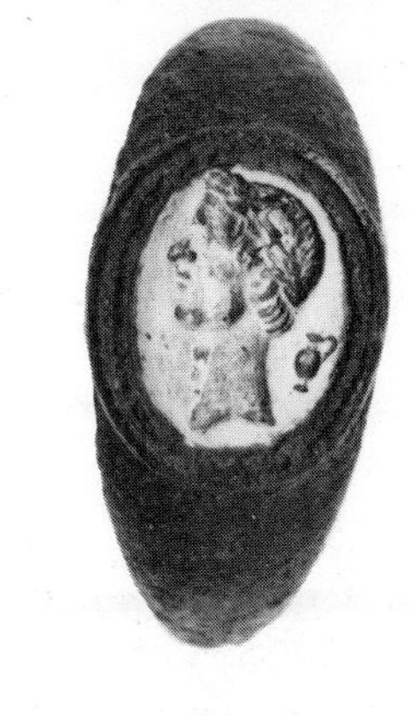

Fig.14 Sextus Pompey. 42-40 BC

presented a traditional Roman image of himself to the world (fig.12). Nevertheless innovations in the use of portraits of Caesar brought the traditions of the Hellenistic kings to Rome. It is not certain that Caesar himself approved the excessive adulation by his party at Rome while he was absent on campaigns. Like other victorious Roman generals before him, Caesar was received as a god in many eastern cities. After his defeat of Pompey at Pharsalus (Thessaly) in 48 BC, statues of him were set up on high bases, sometimes in the company of the goddess Roma, sometimes with Victoria, the personification of victory, and sometimes in a chariot, the symbol of military triumph. After the final defeat of Republican factions at Thapsus in north Africa (46 BC), a bronze portrait of Caesar, accompanied by a globe and a chariot, was set up on the Capitol at Rome facing the statue of Jupiter. In 45 BC, Caesar was presented to the Roman people as the new Romulus: his ivory portrait was carried in a litter (*ferculum*) and placed on a platform (*pulvinar*), which, like the litter, was normally reserved for the images and symbols of the gods.

Important changes in Roman coin portraiture also took place under Caesar. Previously Romans had only been portrayed posthumously on the coin issues of their descendants, but early in 44 BC Caesar had a Senatorial decree passed that he should be portrayed on the coinage, and his portrait duly appeared within his lifetime (fig.13a). This represented an important shift of emphasis, from advertising an ancestor to glorifying oneself, like a Hellenistic king. But Caesar's portrait did not have the explicit symbol of kingship, the diadem, which appeared on some of the imaginary portraits of the ancient Roman kings on first-century BC coins. Caesar preferred a wreath - probably the golden crown or wreath decorated with gems worn by triumphant generals. Thus Caesar behaved like a king but eschewed the title, blending the practice of Hellenistic kings with elements from Roman tradition.

Although most of Caesar's coin portraits were issued after his death, his image appeared on the coins of some Greek cities, for example Nicaea, as early as 48/7 BC (fig.13b). Hitherto, only kings had been thus honoured, and the assimilation of Caesar to Hellenistic kings was confirmed by the type of portrait: in contrast to the later Roman issues, the Nicaean coins have an idealised profile and upward glance, characteristic features of Hellenistic royal portraits.

Caesar's innovations in portraiture set the pattern for the ensuing decade of civil wars. Following the defeat of the assassins led by Brutus (42 BC), the main contenders for leadership at Rome all used portraiture in a similar way. They placed their own portraits on coins used to pay their troops. Octavian and Antony strengthened this appeal to their soldiers' loyalty with posthumous portraits of Caesar. Sextus Pompey used the portrait of his father Pompey in the same way. As there were huge numbers of men under arms the production of coins was vastly increased, and the previous virtual monopoly of the mint of Rome was replaced by widespread minting throughout the Mediterranean - in Spain, Africa, Greece and Asia Minor. The result was a corresponding increase in the numbers of portraits in circulation.

Most of the portraits of this period concentrated on presenting the personal characteristics of their subjects, (fig.14), sometimes rendered in a rather severe style (fig.15). Some portraits of Pompey showed him as Neptune. One statue of Mark Antony, now in the Cairo Museum, showed him as Zeus (fig.16). Wearing the aegis on his shoulders, he was portrayed in the pose created by Lysippos for the young Alexander. Despite the superhuman form of this statue, Antony looks heavy and almost grotesque, a characteristic that is also apparent in his later coin portraits (fig.17).

The reference to Alexander may be explained by the establishment of Antony's court at Alexandria following his marriage to Cleopatra of Egypt. This alliance was construed by Octavian and his supporters as a threat from the east to the existence of Rome. On this pretext the battle of Actium was fought in 31 BC. The victor, Octavian, proclaimed himself the defender of the cause of Italy against the east. Images redolent of kingship became discredited. Octavian subsequently created not only a new political order at Rome, but also a new image for himself as its leader.

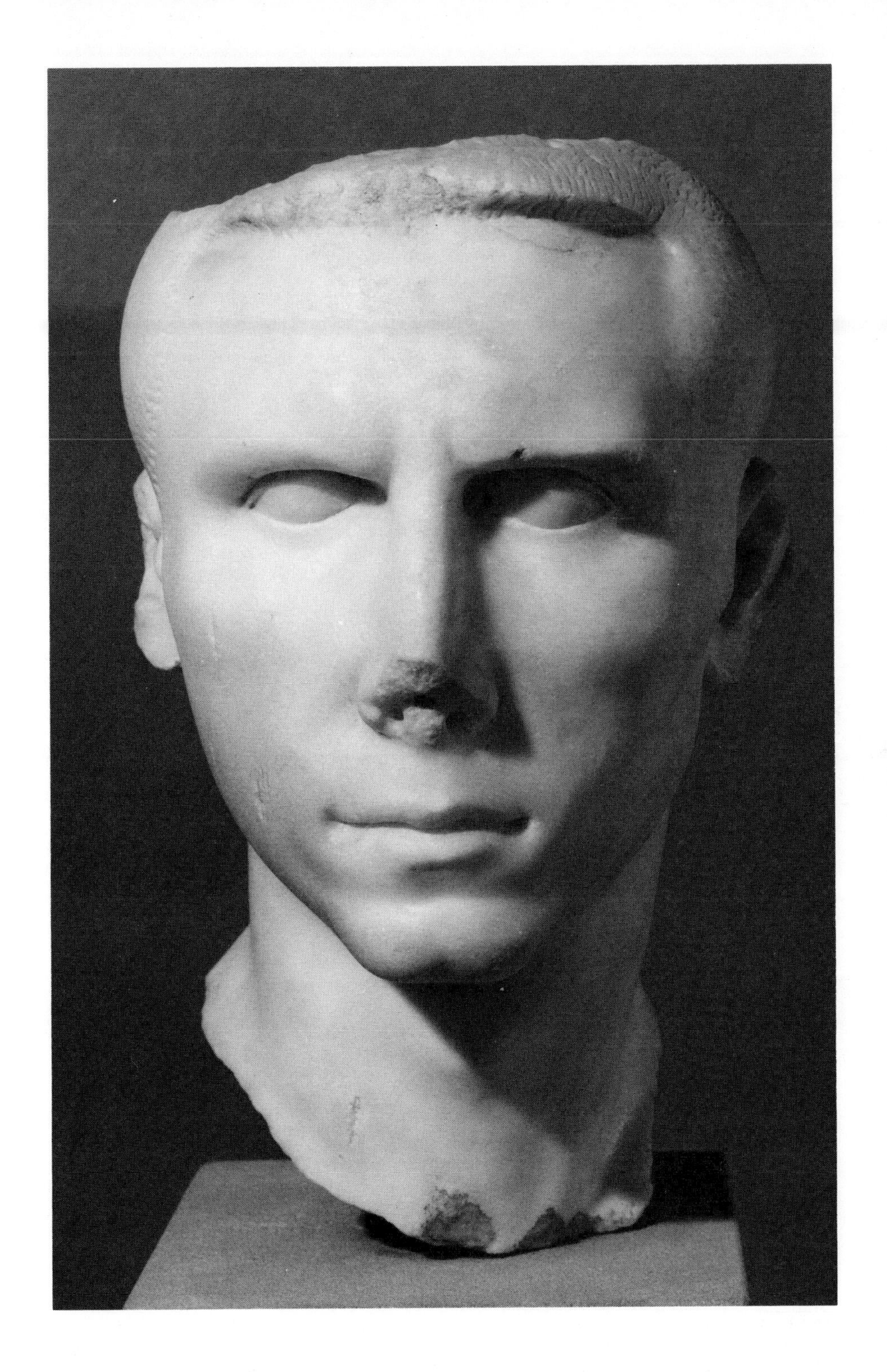

Fig.15 Portrait head of a Roman. c.40–30 BC

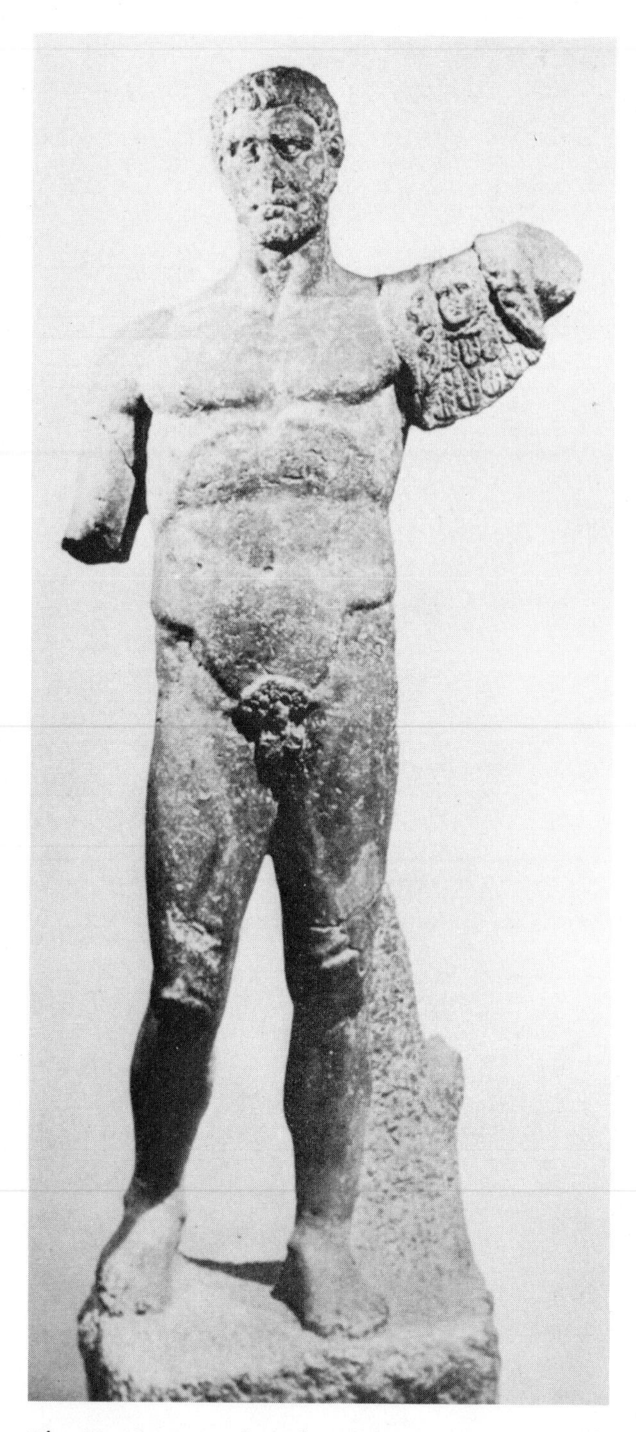

Fig.16 Statue of Mark Antony. c.35-31 BC

Fig.17
Mark Antony. 34 BC

AUGUSTUS

After defeating Antony, Octavian was master of the Roman world. In 27 BC he took the name Augustus. Claiming that he had restored the Republic, he established a new political order, which he himself directed from a position of unrivalled influence.

Augustus appreciated the need for both written and visual presentation of the new order. Realising the dangers of a personal cult, which had been suggested by certain rites and ceremonies introduced to Rome by admirers of Julius Caesar (p.13), he took steps to control the use of images.

Augustus created a new portrait type for himself, intended to present him in an appropriately modest light as *princeps*, first citizen of the restored Republic. He imposed restrictions on the use of his image, allowing some Greek cities with traditions of ruler worship to build temples dedicated to him with the goddess Roma, while refusing to allow temples in places where Roman sentiment might be offended.

The most important of these was Rome itself, where the new policy was inaugurated in spectacular fashion with the destruction and melting down of eighty silver statues of Augustus. The proceeds were dedicated to Apollo in his temple on the Palatine, and the act was proudly recorded in Augustus' own account of his achievements (the *Res Gestae*, see p.27). The use of silver was considered inappropriate for images of living persons, and should be reserved for the gods. Augustus did not disapprove of the statues as such.

Unlike Caesar, Augustus did not permit his statue to be carried in religious processions, and he did not sit on a golden throne. Such marks of divinity were freely conferred on princes of the Augustan house (p.27), but only after their deaths. The controversial divine honours decreed for Caesar were thus neutralised by reserving them for the dead. Augustus himself, if anything enhanced by his rejection of divine honours from over-zealous admirers, enjoyed the reflected glory of deification through his relationship to Caesar.

Augustus' carefully orchestrated propaganda campaign embraced every aspect of political, military and religious life. Three aspects of visual propaganda seem paramount: the development of his personal image as first citizen; the advertising of this, and of his personal qualities and achievements, to the provinces; and the justification of his personal position in public monuments such as his new Forum and the Ara Pacis (p.29).

Fig.18a Octavian. 38 BC

Fig.18b Head from a statue of Octavian. c.38 BC

FROM OCTAVIAN TO AUGUSTUS

Octavian's portrait first appeared on coins of 43 BC (when he was only 19) and after about a year of initial variation his image settled down to a type that, despite some development, remained basically the same for several years, until about 36 BC (fig.18a). This first image was characterised by an extremely youthful appearance and by the constant presence of a beard, which Octavian grew as an expression of grief at his adoptive father's murder: the image represented him as Caesar's son and heir. Few sculpted portraits of this type have survived; one is a head (fig. 18b) from Arles, a colony founded by Julius Caesar.

At first Octavian owed everything to his adoption by Caesar and his consequent use of the name 'Caesar', as Antony sneeringly remarked, but sometime between 35 and 30 BC a new image was chosen, presumably because it was no longer sufficient to be Caesar's heir (fig.19a). The new image also appeared in sculpted portraits (fig.19b), whose exact date of introduction is similarly uncertain. Octavian is shown with the hair above his forehead brushed to one side in lively fashion, his head turned aside, and the muscles of his brow contracted to convey an impression of tension and energy. This type followed the tradition established by Hellenistic rulers: a number of royal coin portraits created about 200 BC showed a comparable youthful idealisation, and the lack of any legend around the head

Fig.19a Octavian. c.33 BC

Fig.19c Antiochus II of Syria. 261-246 BC

Fig.19b Head of Octavian from La Alcudia, Majorca. c.35-30 BC

(unusual in Roman coinage) suggests that Octavian's coin engravers were using such Hellenistic models. As with Julius Caesar, the diadem was omitted, but the clear implication here is that Octavian was placing himself in the tradition of the great Hellenistic kings (fig.19c). Such regal affectations, however, were combined with his personal features: the long neck, the rather pointed features and bone structure, and the small mouth with narrow lips.

Most surviving portraits of Augustus derive from a type created after the establishment of the principate in 27 BC and spread throughout the empire, almost certainly through the means of portable three-dimensional casts, from which copies could be made. The new type reveals the idealisation of Augustus' public image (fig.20a). The head is turned to the front, losing the animation that characterised earlier portraits. The hairstyle is less lively, the locks falling directly on to the forehead. The face has assumed idealised proportions. It is not even possible to tell his age.

Augustus proclaimed that he had restored the Republic: he now selected his image from the repertoire of idealised sculpture created long before in the democratic Greek city-states. While he presented himself as no more than first citizen, his portraits suggested a nobility of body and spirit that set him apart from others.

Fig.20a *Cast of the head of Augustus from Prima Porta*
Fig.20b *Head of the spear-carrier of Polykleitos copied in a herm. c.30 BC*

The debt to Greece can be gauged by a comparison of the statue of Augustus from the villa of his wife Livia at Prima Porta, just outside Rome, with the Doryphoros (spear-carrier) created by the sculptor Polykleitos in about 440 BC. A herm made by the Athenian sculptor Apollonios in about 30 BC was copied from the head of the Doryphoros (fig.20b). The herm, found in Italy and now in the National Museum, Naples, closely resembles the head of the Prima Porta statue in the pose, the proportions of the face, the arrangement of the hair and in the stylised rendering of individual features. The body of the Doryphoros itself was modelled in accordance with a strict system of idealised proportions; it may have served as the master statue for the 'canon' or system of proportions known to have been devised by Polykleitos.

Beneath the armour, the form of the body of the statue of Augustus from Prima Porta seems to have been based on an idealised system of proportions very similar to that devised by Polykleitos. Augustan rhetoricians (some of whom were closely associated with the court of the *princeps*) pronounced that works of art produced in fifth-century Greece were endowed with sublime and honourable qualities. The Flavian writer Quintilian, using a pre-Augustan source, actually implied that the spear-carrier of Polykleitos was the embodiment of the Roman ideal of a serious and pious man (*vir gravis et sanctus*).

Fig.21a Statue of Augustus from the villa of Livia at Prima Porta. c.20-17 BC
Fig.21b Detail of the breastplate from Fig.21a

The statue from Prima Porta is probably a contemporary marble copy of a bronze original, now lost. Augustus appears as a general addressing his troops (fig.21a). He wears a cuirass and a purple ceremonial cloak (*paludamentum*) over the skirt of his tunic. The front of the cuirass records the return to Rome in 20 BC of standards lost to the Parthians at the battle of Carrhae in 53 BC (fig.21b). The statue was probably created in the course of celebrations of Augustus' great diplomatic achievement (20-17 BC). The recovery of the standards, a success still fresh in popular memory, is shown as a cosmic event over which the gods had presided: Augustus' supremacy over the known world is also apparent. There are hints that he was superhuman: the cupid on a dolphin, introduced to support the leg, is a reference to Venus, who, as Venus Genetrix, was the divine ancestress and patron of the Julian family. Augustus' feet are left bare, a state of undress more appropriate to a Greek hero than a Roman general.

An earlier bronze head of Augustus (fig.22), now in the British Museum, was found at Meroë in the Sudan, beyond the Roman imperial frontier. It was probably plundered during Ethiopian raids on the settlements of Philae, Elephantine and Syene (Assuan) in Roman Egypt. It was discovered deliberately concealed in front of the entrance to a temple erected by the Ethiopians to celebrate the success of the raids, which took place in 25-21 BC.

This portrait clearly derives from the type created after the principate was established in 27 BC, although it was evidently made by an artist trained in the Hellenistic tradition. The persistence of this local tradition is apparent in a miniature turquoise head from Egypt that probably represents the emperor Tiberius (fig.22b). While obviously portraying a different person, it is uncannily reminiscent of the Meroë head.

Fig.22a Bronze head of Augustus from Meroë. c.25-21 BC

Fig.22b Miniature turquoise head of Tiberius. AD 14-37

Since Augustus' position was not defined through a single office, but rested on an accumulation of traditional honours and magistracies, no statue type was created for Augustus that showed him in a new role. Instead he was shown performing a number of traditional Republican duties which exemplified his wish to return to old Republican ways. A number of surviving statues show him wearing the toga, a garment that had gone out of fashion among the well-to-do at Rome, to be replaced by Greek styles of dress. The toga could indicate social or official status through coloured stripes or insignia. Augustus could appear as consul, his toga bordered with bright red stripes, or as a triumphant general wearing the purple toga shot through with gold thread. He could appear as a pious citizen performing sacrifice, or attending a religious ceremony, with part of the toga drawn up to veil his head (fig.23).

Fig.23 Augustus veiled as Pontifex Maximus

Fig.24 The oak crown 'for saving citizens'

Fig.25 Augustus. c.2 BC

Fig.26a&b Silver denarius of Augustus copied by a bronze coin (Fig.26c&d) of Leptis Magna

From 27 BC some portraits showed Augustus wearing the *corona civica,* a crown of oak leaves traditionally awarded for saving a fellow-citizen or soldier from death. The crown appears on coins with the legend 'for saving citizens' (fig. 24). The relationship between rescuer and rescued was paternal, and Augustus' appropriation of the oak crown (henceforth it was permitted to no-one else except in a traditional military context) reflected his paternalistic view of his stewardship of the Roman state, which he claimed he himself had rescued from the disastrous effects of the recent civil wars. This paternalism reached a climax with the title 'father of his country'(*pater patriae*)in 2 BC.

On coins Augustus' portrait shows a gradual transition from an image derived from Hellenistic ruler portraiture (fig.19a) to one which, like the sculpted portraits, showed him as first citizen (fig.25). The base of the neck became flatter and the back of the neck straightened out as he lost the upturned gaze, while the hair, in later portraits always decorated with a wreath, became more ordered. These changes had taken place in the west by about 15/10 BC; in the east, as the silver coinage of Antioch shows, they were not complete until some ten or fifteen years later. This eastern preference for the earlier type of portrait reflects the local strength of Hellenistic traditions: the image of the emperor as a Hellenistic ruler was evidently allowed to remain current in the absence of the need to respond to public opinion at Rome.

The importance of Augustan portraits can be judged from the number of surviving examples. Only some thirty sculpted portraits of Caesar are known, compared with at least 250 of Augustus (map 1). A similar picture is evident from the bronze coinage of the cities of the empire. Under Caesar and during the civil wars few cities had used portraits of Roman public figures instead of the usual deities, but under Augustus the number increased to at least 136 (map 2), and many of them issued coins bearing his portrait on a number of occasions. Unfortunately this dramatic change cannot be dated, but as with sculpture, most coin portraits seem to originate after 20 BC, a date suggested by the gold and silver coins used as models by engravers who worked for a particular city such as Lepcis Magna in Africa (fig.26a-d), or Aezani in Asia Minor, or for groups of cities such as those near Mt. Salbace in south-west Asia Minor (Apollonia, Attuda, Cidrama, Heraclea, Dionysopolis, Hierapolis, Laodicea, Siblia and Tripolis). As well as adopting the emperor's portrait, many cities used designs for coin reverses which referred to Augustus: for example, the capricorn, the emperor's birthsign, or his grandsons Gaius and Lucius Caesar.

The explosion in the number of Augustan portraits attests a concerted propaganda campaign aimed at dominating all aspects of civil, religious, economic and military life with Augustus' person. His image stood in forums and temples, on monuments and coins and was carried into battle with the standards. It also occurred in more humble con-

Fig.27a The deified Augustus with a radiate crown

Fig.27b Posthumous portrait of Augustus

Fig.28a&b Head of Octavian with figure of Victory on reverse

Fig.28c&d Bust of Victory with figure of Octavian on reverse

texts, even as the decoration on gaming tokens, and we may imagine that, as later in the second century, the emperor's image could be seen 'on moneychangers' tables, in stalls, in shops, hanging in the eaves, in entrance halls, in windows - everywhere' (Fronto).

After his death in AD 14, Augustus was declared divine (Divus Augustus), as his adoptive father Julius Caesar had been before him in 42 BC (Divus Julius). His statues were no longer honorary portraits of the first citizen but images of a deity. Visible symbols of his deification included a radiate crown (fig.27a) or a star mounted on his head.

Many posthumous statues were heroic or colossal in scale (fig.27b), and some showed him nude or semi-nude, often in a pose that was used for statues of Jupiter, yet the heads remained based on the portraits created during his reign. Most of these statues were created during the reigns of his successors Tiberius, Gaius (Caligula) and Claudius, to whom the memory of Augustus' achievements had a direct relevance.

AUGUSTUS' USE OF COIN PROPAGANDA

'They handed him a silver piece. Jesus asked, "Whose head is this and whose inscription?" "Caesar's," they replied.' (Matthew 22).

In the Roman world coins offered perhaps the best medium for visual propaganda, not least because their frequent handling ensured the constant presentation of their designs to those whose loyalty mattered: people in cities who used money in their transactions, and soldiers who were paid directly in coin. In the first century BC coins had often been used as propaganda, particularly after the return of Pompey to Rome, but their allusions were sometimes indirect and obscure. Augustus exploited their potential by systematically and often explicitly using coins to promote his message.

At the end of the civil wars, Augustus used coins to publish his manifesto: peace and victory under the protection of patron divinities. One group of coins, issued before 27 BC, had such a combination (fig.28a-d).

Obverse head	Reverse figure	Obverse head	Reverse figure
Octavian	Peace	Peace	Octavian
Octavian	Venus	Venus	Octavian
Octavian	Victory	Victory	Octavian

Later two themes dominated: the establishment of a dynasty (and the consequent problem of the succession) and his achievement as *Princeps*. In conveying the second his coinage shows a similarity of content with the *Res Gestae* (see p.29), an inscription set up on his Mausoleum and elsewhere after his death, but probably drafted by Augustus himself much earlier, and updated until his death in AD 14. The

Fig.29a Augustus restoring the Republic

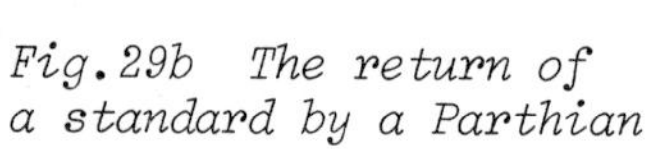

Fig.29b The return of a standard by a Parthian

Fig.29c Victory crowning Augustus in an elephant chariot on a viaduct

Fig.29d The laurel branches and oak crown fixed by the door of Augustus' house

inscription therefore represents Augustus' own view of what he had achieved, and his coins naturally reflect his personal choice.

Both the inscription and the coins recorded the end of the civil wars, referring indirectly to Augustus' defeats of Sextus Pompey and Antony, and propagated his favourite political slogans: the restoration of peace and liberty and of the Republic (fig.29a). The subsequent history of his reign, as seen through his eyes, dwells on two themes: his military and diplomatic successes (the capture of Armenia, or the recovery of the Parthian and Gallic military standards: fig.29b), and his financial generosity to the state: how he had often helped the treasury, paid for road construction (fig.29c) and public entertainments. These achievements and acts of generosity were rewarded with a series of extravagant honours: the title 'Augustus', the setting up of laurel branches and an oak crown outside his house (fig.29d), the golden shield of valour and the title 'Father of his Country'. References to these honours frequently appeared on his coins.

The *Res Gestae*, the coins and the deliberate propagation of the portrait all gave the same emphasis to the person of the *Princeps*. His allies and supporters, to whom he owed everything, were virtually ignored: the conclusion of thirty years of civil war and the institution of a new political order were presented as the achievement of Augustus alone.

Fig.30 Reconstruction of the Mausoleum of Augustus. 28 BC

THE MAUSOLEUM OF AUGUSTUS (fig.30)

The *Res Gestae* were inscribed on two bronze tablets fixed to two columns at the entrance to Augustus' mausoleum. This round monumental tomb was built in 28 BC, and it is ironic that at the very time that Augustus was dressing up his monarchy with the 'Restoration of the Republic', he was engaged in the building of this colossal monument in the Campus Martius as if to mark the foundation of his imperial dynasty. The Campus Martius had already become the place of burial for those like Julius Caesar who were granted a public funeral, but the mausoleum was on an unprecedented scale (it was 88 metres in diameter) and was from the beginning intended for the burial of all Augustus' family and heirs. When completed the mausoleum epitomised his own position and that of his family in the new order, his statue surmounting the huge mound. The decision to build the mausoleum at Rome may have been intended to counter Antony's plans for his own mausoleum at Alexandria, and attests Octavian's early intention of establishing an imperial dynasty.

AUGUSTAN PUBLIC MONUMENTS

Roman sculpture was always designed for a specific setting. Most sculptures were intended to be seen as part of a group that, taken together, either told a story or presented a particular message. Nowhere is this more clearly expressed than in the Forum of Augustus, completed in 2 BC (fig.31), and located in a densely populated district in the centre of Rome, north-east of the Forum begun by Julius Caesar. According to Suetonius, Augustus liked to boast that he found Rome a city of brick and left it a city of marble, but he restrained the grandeur of his Forum to forestall objections from displaced residents. Later emperors were to show no such restraint.

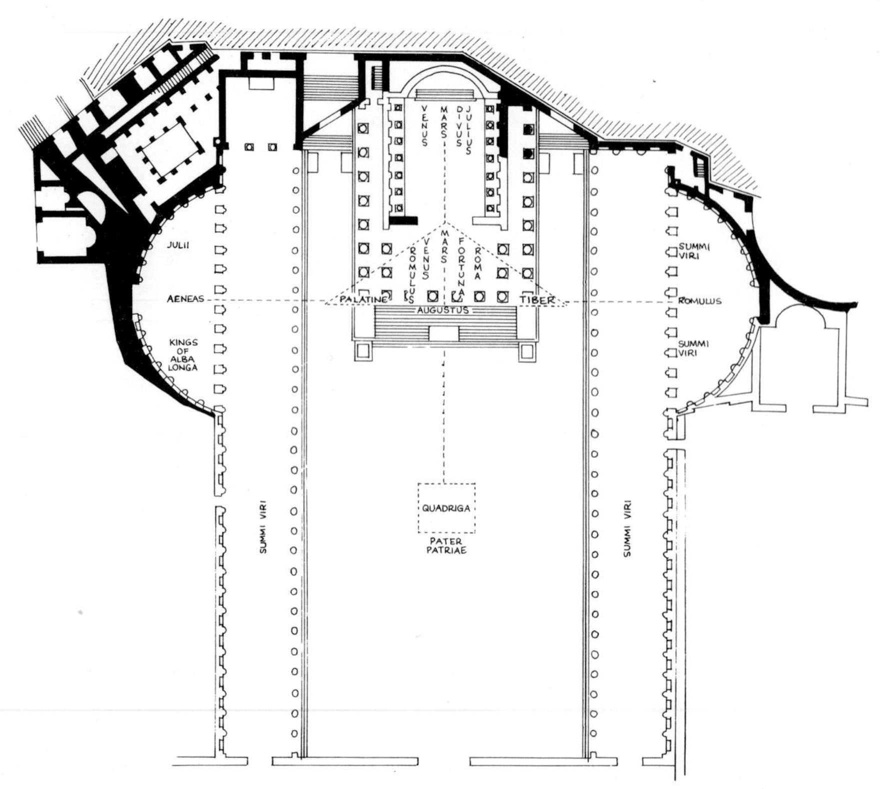

Fig.31 Forum of Augustus, dedicated in 2 BC. Plan showing location of the statues

Fig.32 Model of the Temple of Mars Ultor with part of the Forum

The new Forum was dominated by a temple dedicated to Mars the Avenger, patron god of wars of just retribution. The temple was set on a high platform (*podium*) approached only at the front by a flight of steps. Before it was a large open space, bounded at the sides by colonnades which opened into semi-circular recesses (*exedrae*) aligned with the front of the temple (fig.32).

The Forum, which resembled the sanctuaries built in Hellenistic royal cities, was adorned with statues that were arranged to illustrate the historical inevitability of Augustus' position as head of state (*princeps*), and to celebrate the acquisition of territory by Rome. Set into niches in the walls of the colonnades were gilded bronze statues of the *summi viri*, the most distinguished generals and statesmen of the Roman Republic. Each stood on a base inscribed with a record of his achievements (*elogium*), recording the merits that had won for the subject a place in this gallery of heroes. These *elogia*, which resembled the *Res Gestae* in style, are also thought to have been composed by Augustus himself.

In one *exedra* stood statues of the fabled kings of Alba Longa, predecessors of the kings of Rome, with members of the family of Julius Caesar. With them too was the Trojan hero Aeneas, a legendary founder of Rome and a Julian ancestor, occupying a central position between the two groups. In the other *exedra*, Republican heroes flanked a statue of Romulus, founder of the city. Exactly half-way between Aeneas and Romulus, set in large letters on the front of the temple, were the names and titles of Augustus. The descent of Romulus through the kings of Alba Longa from Venus' son Aeneas had been documented in a work published by L. Julius Caesar, the family historian; Caesar himself had asserted that his family was descended from Venus. Thus Augustus was shown as the natural successor to the popular legendary founders of Rome, Aeneas and Romulus. The link was underlined by the statues inside the temple; the cult statue of Mars, father of Romulus, was flanked by one of the deified Julius Caesar, the father of Augustus, and one of Venus, the mother of Aeneas and the patron goddess and ancestress of the Julian family.

Augustus himself recorded that his Forum had been constructed from the proceeds of military spoils. Indeed, its militaristic nature was expressed as strongly as the historical. The legionary standards lost to the Parthians by Crassus in 53 BC and recovered through Augustus' diplomacy in 20 BC were displayed in the Temple of Mars the Avenger (fig.33). The Augustan poet Ovid remarked that, immediately on entry, the eye of the visitor was assailed by weapons captured by Roman soldiers from all countries of the known world. The most prominent monument was a four-horse chariot (*quadriga*) awarded to Augustus by the Senate on completion of the Forum in 2 BC. The *princeps* was probably shown as a triumphant general mounted in the chariot, on the point of receiving a crown from the personification of

Victory. On the podium was inscribed the title 'Father of his Country' (*Pater Patriae*) awarded in the same year, and a list of his military achievements (in reality those of his subordinates, since Augustus was not a distinguished commander in the field). The exact location of the *quadriga* is unknown, but it must have been set somewhere in the open space in front of the temple, as yet unexcavated.

The architectural decoration, too, was an exercise in propaganda. The attic above the colonnade was decorated with shields set in panels divided by projecting caryatids. The bosses of the shields took the form of various deities, including Jupiter Ammon, with whom Alexander the Great had become identified after his death. Caryatids, here modelled on those of the Erechtheion in Athens, had come to symbolise servitude - in this context, that of the Greek world at the hands of Rome. The Forum was covered with veneers of coloured marble, quarried from many places in the empire, another sign of Roman domination over the Mediterranean world.

No less significant was the display of Greek works of art that had been brought to Rome. Augustus himself brought the archaic cult statue of Athena Alea from Tegea in the Peloponnese. He also displayed two paintings of Alexander by Apelles, one showing him as victor accompanied by Nike (Victory) and the Dioscuri, Castor and Pollux; the other as bringer of peace after battle, a clear allusion to the peaceful conclusion of civil wars at Rome. The messages seem only too obvious, yet fifty years later the emperor Claudius felt it necessary to substitute the features of the deified Augustus for those of Alexander.

In his Forum, Augustus validated his claim to be Caesar's heir. But this was no mere historical monument: the Forum became a centre for important ceremonies of state. Within the temple of Mars, the Senate held debates on future military commitments and peace treaties; they also received here foreign heads of state. Provincial governors sacrificed at the Altar of Mars before assuming their posts. Triumphant generals dedicated their spoils of victory here, and newly eligible members of leading Roman families were inscribed in the military lists. The Forum of Augustus absorbed some of the functions of the temple of Jupiter on the Capitol; it represented Augustus' sphere of government, just as the Roman Forum represented that of the Republican Senate and assembly. As such it was a living structure, despite the strongly historical tone of its decoration; and, as history continued to be made by members of Augustus' family, so in turn were their statues dedicated among the *summi viri* of Rome.

While the Forum of Augustus commemorated military achievement, peace was celebrated in the Altar of Augustan Peace (*Ara Pacis Augustae*). It was voted by the Senate in July, 13 BC as a thank-offering on Augustus' safe return after some years in Spain and Gaul. It was finally dedicated in the Campus Martius near the Tiber in January, 9 BC. The

Fig.33 Temple of Mars Ultor with standard recovered from the Parthians

altar was set on a stepped podium and surrounded by a high precinct wall, which could be entered from two sides (fig.34). The inner face of the wall was decorated in a manner appropriate to a sacrificial altar, showing garlands of fruit and flowers slung between bulls' skulls, which were set above a marble replica of a wooden fence. The latter may have been a monumental version of a wooden fence built for the consecration ceremony in 13 BC. On the east and west walls, flanking the entrances, were carved allegorical figures alluding to the legendary origins and the contemporary and future prosperity of Rome. On the lower register was a frieze of acanthus leaves, carved in the Hellenistic manner and enlivened with animal figures. The upper register on the outer faces of the north and south walls was occupied by two rows of figures moving in a procession towards the western entrance to the altar. The scene is generally interpreted as a record of the consecration ceremony. The concept is reminiscent of the frieze on the Parthenon at Athens, and the overall design of the monument is based on that of the Altar of the Twelve Gods, built in the Athenian Agora during the late fifth century BC.

The Augustan altar, however, had something new. Instead of the participants being segregated by sex and function as they were on the frieze of the Parthenon, they were shown in family groups, often accompanied by young children. These were not necessarily their own children, but could be nephews or nieces, or even Gaulish princes, whose futures rested with Rome (fig.35). Members of the imperial house were thus shown in their role as heads of families, probably to serve as examples to other Romans at a time when Augustus was formulating laws to encourage marriage and raise the birth rate among Roman citizens.

The role and social position of the members of the procession can be identified through their dress. Augustus himself appears with his toga drawn over his head as was proper before performing a sacrifice. He stands at the head

Fig.34 Reconstruction of the Ara Pacis. 13-9 BC

Fig.35 Family groups from the procession frieze of the Ara Pacis

of a group of priests, which included the priest of the cult of the deified Julius Caesar and Roman magistrates (fig.36). A woman, probably his daughter Julia, appears in the fringed shawl normally worn by widows. The young Domitius, son of Augustus' niece Antonia, wears an amulet (*bulla*) and the toga with a purple stripe (*toga praetexta*) worn by children of senators. He tugs on the ceremonial cloak (*paludamentum*) of his uncle, Augustus' younger stepson Drusus. The Gaulish princes can be distinguished by their long hair and necklets (torques). Although the arrangement and decoration of the altar derive from earlier models, the presence of children on such a monument for the first time symbolised the future hopes of the Augustan house, the new order that Augustus had established, and the universal peace and prosperity he had brought.

Fig.36 The Ara Pacis: priests and members of the Imperial Family

PRIVATE PORTRAITS IN THE AGE OF AUGUSTUS

The cultural preferences of Augustan court circles showed a taste for a refined rendering of themes and motifs drawn from classical and hellenistic art and literature. In art this taste was not confined to portraiture, but extended to all the applied arts, such as the silverware, fine pottery, paintings and even the bronze and marble furniture that graced the homes of the wealthy.

Some Roman patrician families, however, retained an ostentatious preference for the severely 'realistic' style of portraiture in traditional use for portraits of their class during the Republic (p. 8 ; fig.37a). Ironically a

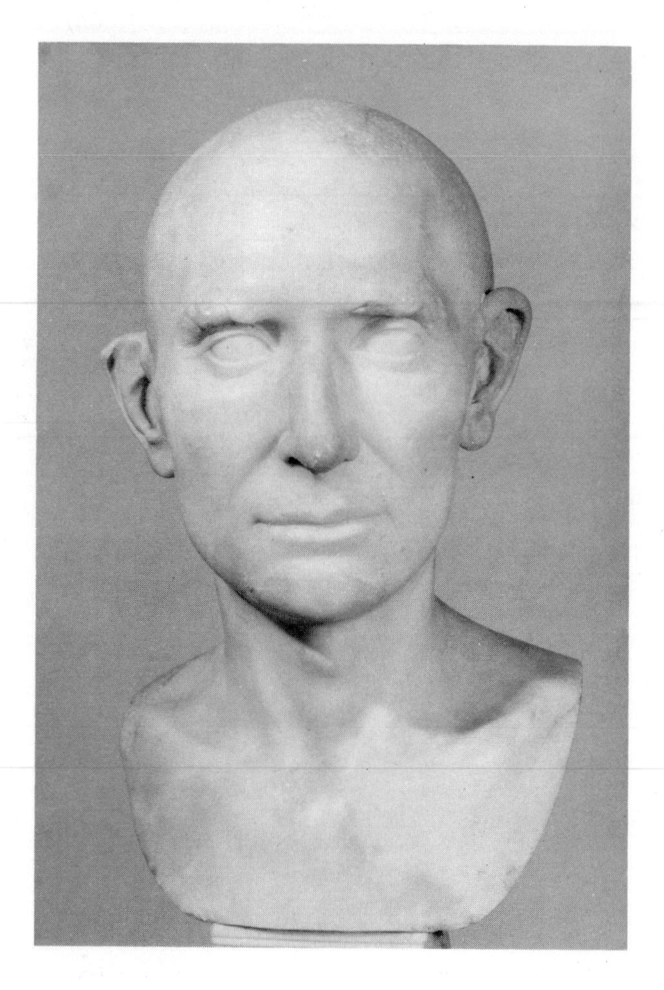

Fig.37a Augustan portrait of a Patrician Roman

Fig.37b   Augustan tomb on the Via Appia with a 'freedmen relief'

new class of patrons favouring this traditional style of portrait had emerged by the beginning of Augustus' reign among the freedmen, former slaves who had bought their own freedom or who had been manumitted by their masters. They were often set up in business by their patrons, who hoped to recoup substantial profits from their investment. A wide field of crafts and professions lay open to freedmen, many of whom were well-educated people from the Greek-speaking east. Some amassed considerable fortunes, and many chose to commemorate their new status (through which their marriages were legitimised and their children became Roman citizens), in framed marble or travertine relief portraits, set in the outside walls of their tombs (fig.37b).

Fig.38 'Freedmen relief': a smith and a carpenter with their tools. c.20-5 BC

Fig.39 'Freedmen relief': L. Ampudius Philomusus and his family

Fig.40 Relief dedicated to Antistius Sarculo and his wife by their freedmen

Since Roman law did not recognise a slave's natural parents, most 'freedmen reliefs' portray the deceased along with their spouses and adult children. Other reliefs show freedmen who had been freed and set up in business together. The emphasis on their present condition and their hopes for the future stands in sharp contrast to the reverence for the past shown in patrician portraits of the Republic.

Celebrating their new-found wealth and respectability, freedmen selected the traditional Roman style for their portraits, camouflaging their alien origins despite the tell-tale evidence of names in the accompanying epitaphs. Most portraits are bust-length: their subjects stare directly to the front and carry no symbols of status, nor do they make complex gestures. The women imitated the distinctive hairstyle of Augustus' empress Livia and his daughter Julia, and some of the younger men wore their hair as Augustus did. But generally they were slow to adopt new fashions, the men retaining the close-shaven Republican hairstyle long after it had gone out of fashion among the aristocracy. Later Augustan reliefs reveal the freedmen in more relaxed poses; sometimes the family groups are modelled on those on the *Ara Pacis* (p.34).

The reliefs were inscribed with the names of the deceased and those of his family or associates who had paid for the tomb. Professions were often recorded: a famous example shows a smith and a carpenter who may have been freed together, with the tools of their trade displayed in the frame around their portraits (fig.38). Another relief shows a man with his wife and daughter, with corn measures (*modii*) set on either side of the picture frame (fig.39). Freedmen sometimes set up portraits of their patrons, such as the fine relief dedicated to Lucius Antistius Sarculo and his wife Antistia Plutia, herself a former slave (fig.40).

Fig.41 Portrait of Tiberius. c.AD 4

The funerary reliefs of freedmen reveal much about the personal histories and the future aspirations of their subjects. The reliefs are not known in significant numbers after the reign of Augustus, but the conventions of Augustan freedmen reliefs were widely adopted by leading citizens of provincial towns for their tombstones.

AUGUSTUS FOUNDS A DYNASTY

Augustus intended to found a ruling dynasty from the very beginning of his reign, as the construction of his mausoleum makes clear (p.29). The difficulty of finding a suitable successor troubled him throughout his life, since his chosen candidates died young. He was finally succeeded by his stepson Tiberius, whom Augustus had not favoured, but whose interests had been unceasingly promoted by his mother Livia, Augustus' third wife.

It was important to familiarise the public, especially the army, with the notion of a ruling family and with the identity of chosen successors. The princes picked to succeed Augustus were made to look like the emperor in their official portraits, a device that reinforced the legitimacy of their claims to rule (compare the successors to Alexander, p. 4). When Tiberius succeeded Augustus in AD 14, he was already fifty, and yet in his official portraits he was made to appear as a younger version of the emperor (fig.41). All the princes of the Julio-Claudian house were portrayed with serene expressions and Augustan hairstyles. Their own identities were so strongly suppressed that it is very difficult to tell them apart without the aid of identifying inscriptions. The portraits of some princes have even been confused with those of Augustus himself.

The portraits of his grandsons Gaius (20 BC - AD 4) and Lucius (17 BC - AD 2) Caesar, the sons of Augustus' close friend and colleague Marcus Agrippa and of his daughter Julia, well illustrate this last point (fig.42a+b). For a long time the portraits of one (which one cannot yet be determined) were thought to represent Augustus as a youth. However, the posthumous creation of a portrait that differs from the known portaits of Octavian seems pointless. The group portraits of Augustus with his two grandsons suggest by their very existence that he may have been the originator of their portrait types. He may even have intended to present them as the new Octavian and the new Augustus. This impression of dynastic ambition is strengthened by the interest that Augustus showed in the education and welfare of the young princes. They accompanied him everywhere; he taught them to read and to swim and to imitate his own handwriting. Augustus even held the consulship in order to preside over their entry into the adult community of Roman citizens (in 5 and 2 BC). Gaius and Lucius were themselves designated for the consulship, the highest Roman public office, at a precocious age. This award was voted to them by the Roman Senate; the order of Roman knights (*equites*) appointed them 'leaders of Roman youth' (*principes iuventutis*),

Fig.42a&b Portraits of Gaius and Lucius Caesar

a role in which they appear on the coinage of Augustus (fig. 43) and for which they received dedications and statues from cities throughout the empire (fig.44). To the grief of Augustus, both Gaius and Lucius died young through accident and illness, and the succession passed to their morose step-father Tiberius, who had been obliged to marry their widowed mother Julia after the death of their father Agrippa in 13 BC.

As consorts of princes and producers of heirs, women now assumed a greater political importance than under the Republic. The women of the imperial family were celebrated posthumously as goddesses through portraits that idealised their virtues (fig.45), a reverence hardly appropriate to the scandalous intrigues and flagrant immorality of some members of Augustus' family. Although their facial appearances are idealised, the women of the Julio-Claudian house can usually be identified through their hairstyles. They

Fig.43 Gaius and Lucius Caesar. Reverse of coin of Augustus. c.2 BC

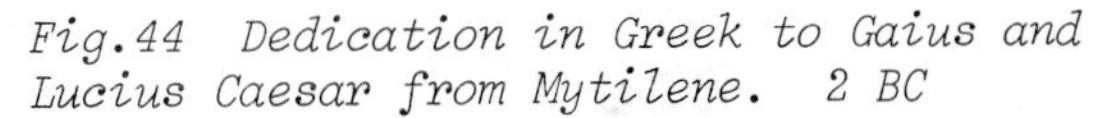

Fig.44 Dedication in Greek to Gaius and Lucius Caesar from Mytilene. 2 BC

sometimes appear in group portraits as a bridge between the generations, emphasising again the consolidation of a royal family, a characteristic of the Macedonian royal house and of the Ptolemies of Egypt (p. 3). Julio-Claudian princes were also portrayed accompanied by their male heirs (fig.46), who personified the continuity of imperial rule. The Julio-Claudian house retained control of the Roman empire until the death of Nero in AD 68.

Augustus ended the *Res Gestae* (p.27) with the laconic note that, at the time of writing, he was in his seventy-sixth year. In the fifty-seven years that had elapsed since the assassination of Caesar, the Roman state had been completely transformed. There has been much comment about the formation of a new political order at Rome, with Augustus at its head. Less has been said of the creation of a new image for a supreme head of state - a 'portrait' which disguised the nature of Augustus' power as effectively as did his cautious policies.

Fig.45 Cameo portraits of Livia as Juno and Julia as Roma
Fig.46 Glass medallion from Colchester: Germanicus with his children, Nero, Drusus III, and Gaius (Caligula) c.AD 23

LIST OF ILLUSTRATIONS

The photographs were provided by the listed museums and galleries, except for the following: nos.16 (B. Bothmer); 19b (DAI Madrid, Inst.Neg. R 1-71-9; Photo P. Witte); 32 (Fototeca Unione); 35, 36 (Alinari).

FURTHER READING

Ancient Sources

Suetonius, *Augustus* (trans. R. Graves, *Lives of the Caesars*, London, 1970).
P. Brunt - J. M. Moore, *Res Gestae Divi Augusti* (text, translation and commentary, Oxford 1967).

Modern Historical Works

ed. S. A. Cook, F. E. Adcock, M. P. Charlesworth, *Cambridge Ancient History* Vol.X. *The Augustan Empire 44 BC - AD 14* (Cambridge 1934).
J. M. Carter, *The Battle of Actium: the rise and triumph of Augustus Caesar* (London 1970).
A. H. M. Jones, *Augustus* (London 1970).
R. Syme, *The Roman Revolution* (Oxford 1939).
S. Weinstock, *Divus Julius* (London 1972).

Portraits

M. Bieber, *Alexander the Great in Greek and Roman Art* (Chicago 1964).
P. Zanker, *Studien zu den Augustus-Porträts 1. Der Actium-Typus* (Abh. Göttingen, 2nd edition 1978).

K. Vierneisel-P. Zanker, *Die Bildnisse des Augustus* (Munich 1979).
D. E. E. Kleiner, *Roman Group Portraiture* (New York 1977).
J. M. C. Toynbee, *Roman Historical Portraits* (London 1978).

Augustan Monuments

P. Zanker, *Forum Augustum* (Wasmuth, Tubingen: undated).
E. Simon, *Ara Pacis Augustae* (Wasmuth, Tubingen: undated).

Coinage

C. H. V. Sutherland, *Coinage in Roman Imperial Policy* (London 1951).
K. Kraft, *Zur Münzprägung des Augustus* (Wiesbaden 1969).
C. H. V. Sutherland - C M Kraay, *Catalogue of Coins of the Roman Empire in the Ashmolean Museum. Part 1: Augustus* (Oxford 1975).
I. Carradice, *Ancient Greek Portrait Coins* (London 1978).

S. Walker - A. Burnett, *Augustus: Handlist of the Exhibition and Supplementary Studies* (London 1981).

ACKNOWLEDGMENTS

The authors thank their colleagues in the Museum and in universities for their help and advice.
The typescript was produced by Marian Vian and the book was designed by Susan Bird, who drew the maps from information supplied by Professor Dr Paul Zanker.

ISBN 0 7141 1270 4
Published by British Museum Publications
46 Bloomsbury Street, London WC1B 3QQ.

Printed in Great Britain by
The Saffron Press, Saffron Walden.

MAP 1

Find spots of portraits of Augustus

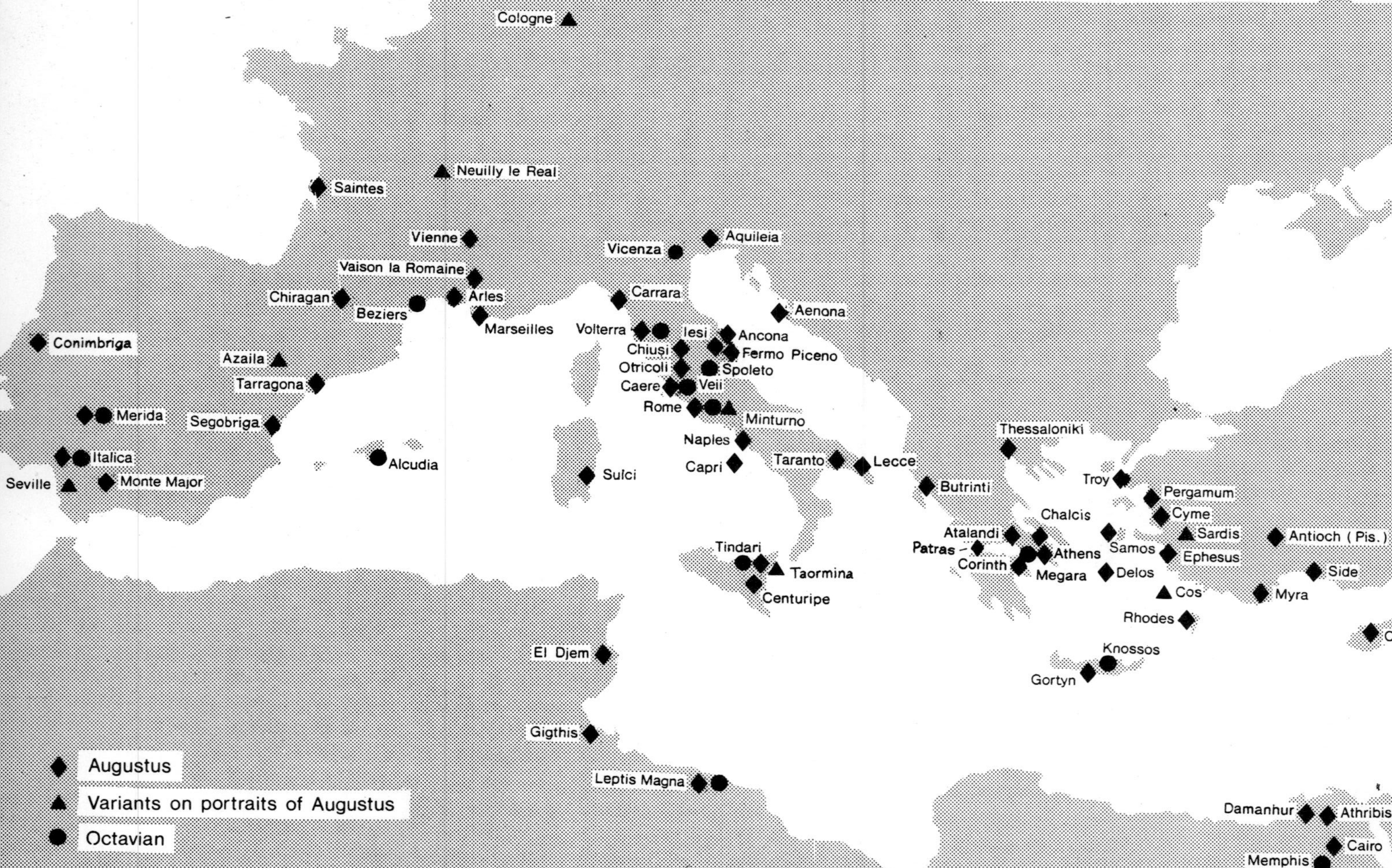